Published by Willow Creek Press, Inc.
P.O. Box 147, Minocqua, Wisconsin 54548

Design: Donnie Rubo
Printed in China

ANIMAL YOGA

ANIMAL YOGA

■ WILLOW CREEK PRESS®

In 1896, tigers at the New Delhi Zoo were observed practicing rudimentary yoga poses within their enclosures. Their astonished keepers encouraged this remarkable behavior and before long they were demonstrating up to seven distinct postures. At the turn of the century several of these tigers were shipped on loan to zoos in the West. Zoo animals throughout the U.S. and Europe quickly noted and mimicked the tigers behavior. This unique practice of yoga is believed to have spread from zoo enclosures to the animal kingdom at large sometime between 1935 and 1942. The rest, as they say, is history.

There are many goals but one path—
the path of compassion.

—Amit Ray

Sun salutations can energize and warm you, even on the darkest, coldest winter day.

—Carol Krucoff

When you find peace within yourself,
you become the kind of person who
can live at peace with others.

—Peace Pilgrim

Your task is not to seek for love,
but merely to seek and find all
the barriers within yourself that
you have built against it.

—Rumi

There is no need for temples, no
need for complicated philosophies.
My brain and my heart are my temples;
my philosophy is kindness.

—Dalai Lama

Without inner peace, outer peace is impossible.

—Geshe Kelsang Gyatso

Mindfulness helps you go home to the present. And every time you go there and recognize a condition of happiness that you have, happiness comes.

—Thich Nhat Hanh

Be a lamp to yourself. Be your
own confidence. Hold to the truth
within yourself as to the only truth.

—Buddha

You cannot travel the path until
you have become the path itself.

—Buddha

Sitting quietly, doing nothing, spring comes, and the grass grows by itself.

—Zen Proverb

Silence is not silent. Silence speaks. It speaks most eloquently. Silence is not still. Silence leads. It leads most perfectly.

—Sri Chinmoy

The part can never be well
unless the whole is well.

—Plato

The body is your temple. Keep it pure
and clean for the soul to reside in.

–B.K.S. Iyengar

You must find the place inside yourself
where nothing is impossible.

—Deepak Chopra

Peace comes from within.

Do not seek it without.

—Buddha

Our bodies are our gardens to
which our wills are gardeners.

—William Shakespeare

In the midst of movement and chaos,
keep stillness inside of you.

—Deepak Chopra

A river cuts through a rock, not because
of its power, but its persistence.

—Unknown

Blessed are the flexible, for they
shall not be bent out of shape.

—Unknown

When the mind is exhausted
of images, it invents its own.

—Gary Snyder

Sometimes you find yourself
in the middle of nowhere, and
sometimes in the middle of
nowhere, you find yourself.

—Unknown

The wise man lets go of all results,
whether good or bad, and is
focused on the action alone.

—Bhagavad Gita

Happiness is a state of
inner fulfillment.

—Matthieu Ricard

Yoga is like music. The rhythm of
the body, the melody of the mind,
and the harmony of the soul
create the symphony of life.

—B.K.S. Iyengar

Have wisdom in your actions
and faith in your merits.

—Yogi Bhajan

Happiness is not a matter of
intensity but of balance, order,
rhythm and harmony.

—Thomas Merton

In our uniquely human capacity of
connect movement with breath and
spiritual meaning, yoga is born.

—Gurmukh Kaur Khalsa